A Month of Mandalas

EGGS

31 Mandalas to Colour

Elle Kaye

This book belongs to:
_____

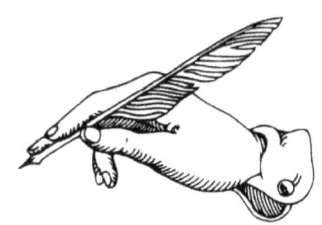

A Month of Mandalas EGGS Colouring BooK

Copyright © 2021 Elle Kaye

All rights reserved. No part of this publication may be reproduced, distributed, or transmitted, in any form, or by any means, including photocopying, recording, or other electronic or mechanical methods.

ISBN: 978-1-7775935-2-0

TODAY'S DATE:

"Once you replace negative thoughts with positive ones, you'll start having positive results." — Willie Nelson

RIGHT NOW I FEEL:

I WOULD LIKE TO FEEL:

AS I COLOUR MY MANDALA, I FOCUS ON TIMES WHEN I FEEL HOW I WOULD LIKE TO FEEL. BY DOING THIS I ATTRACT MORE OF IT INTO MY FUTURE DAYS.

THE BEST THING THAT HAPPENED TODAY:

THINGS I ACCOMPLISHED TODAY, BIG AND SMALL:

TODAY'S DATE:

"Once you replace negative thoughts with positive ones, you'll start having positive results." — Willie Nelson

RIGHT NOW I FEEL:

I WOULD LIKE TO FEEL:

AS I COLOUR MY MANDALA, I FOCUS ON TIMES WHEN I FEEL HOW I WOULD LIKE TO FEEL. BY DOING THIS I ATTRACT MORE OF IT INTO MY FUTURE DAYS.

THE BEST THING THAT HAPPENED TODAY:

THINGS I ACCOMPLISHED TODAY, BIG AND SMALL:

TODAY'S DATE:

"Once you replace negative thoughts with positive ones, you'll start having positive results." — Willie Nelson

RIGHT NOW I FEEL:

I WOULD LIKE TO FEEL:

AS I COLOUR MY MANDALA, I FOCUS ON TIMES WHEN I FEEL HOW I WOULD LIKE TO FEEL. BY DOING THIS I ATTRACT MORE OF IT INTO MY FUTURE DAYS.

THE BEST THING THAT HAPPENED TODAY:

THINGS I ACCOMPLISHED TODAY, BIG AND SMALL:

TODAY'S DATE:

"Once you replace negative thoughts with positive ones, you'll start having positive results." — Willie Nelson

RIGHT NOW I FEEL:

I WOULD LIKE TO FEEL:

AS I COLOUR MY MANDALA, I FOCUS ON TIMES WHEN I FEEL HOW I WOULD LIKE TO FEEL. BY DOING THIS I ATTRACT MORE OF IT INTO MY FUTURE DAYS.

THE BEST THING THAT HAPPENED TODAY:

THINGS I ACCOMPLISHED TODAY, BIG AND SMALL:

TODAY'S DATE:

"Once you replace negative thoughts with positive ones, you'll start having positive results." — Willie Nelson

RIGHT NOW I FEEL:

I WOULD LIKE TO FEEL:

AS I COLOUR MY MANDALA, I FOCUS ON TIMES WHEN I FEEL HOW I WOULD LIKE TO FEEL. BY DOING THIS I ATTRACT MORE OF IT INTO MY FUTURE DAYS.

THE BEST THING THAT HAPPENED TODAY:

THINGS I ACCOMPLISHED TODAY, BIG AND SMALL:

TODAY'S DATE:

"Once you replace negative thoughts with positive ones, you'll start having positive results." — Willie Nelson

RIGHT NOW I FEEL:

I WOULD LIKE TO FEEL:

AS I COLOUR MY MANDALA, I FOCUS ON TIMES WHEN I FEEL HOW I WOULD LIKE TO FEEL. BY DOING THIS I ATTRACT MORE OF IT INTO MY FUTURE DAYS.

THE BEST THING THAT HAPPENED TODAY:

THINGS I ACCOMPLISHED TODAY, BIG AND SMALL:

TODAY'S DATE:

"Once you replace negative thoughts with positive ones, you'll start having positive results." —Willie Nelson

RIGHT NOW I FEEL:

I WOULD LIKE TO FEEL:

AS I COLOUR MY MANDALA, I FOCUS ON TIMES WHEN I FEEL HOW I WOULD LIKE TO FEEL. BY DOING THIS I ATTRACT MORE OF IT INTO MY FUTURE DAYS.

THE BEST THING THAT HAPPENED TODAY:

THINGS I ACCOMPLISHED TODAY, BIG AND SMALL:

TODAY'S DATE:

"Once you replace negative thoughts with positive ones, you'll start having positive results." — Willie Nelson

RIGHT NOW I FEEL:

I WOULD LIKE TO FEEL:

AS I COLOUR MY MANDALA, I FOCUS ON TIMES WHEN I FEEL HOW I WOULD LIKE TO FEEL. BY DOING THIS I ATTRACT MORE OF IT INTO MY FUTURE DAYS.

THE BEST THING THAT HAPPENED TODAY:

THINGS I ACCOMPLISHED TODAY, BIG AND SMALL:

TODAY'S DATE:

"Once you replace negative thoughts with positive ones, you'll start having positive results." — Willie Nelson

RIGHT NOW I FEEL:

I WOULD LIKE TO FEEL:

AS I COLOUR MY MANDALA, I FOCUS ON TIMES WHEN I FEEL HOW I WOULD LIKE TO FEEL. BY DOING THIS I ATTRACT MORE OF IT INTO MY FUTURE DAYS.

THE BEST THING THAT HAPPENED TODAY:

THINGS I ACCOMPLISHED TODAY, BIG AND SMALL:

TODAY'S DATE:

"Once you replace negative thoughts with positive ones, you'll start having positive results." — Willie Nelson

RIGHT NOW I FEEL:

I WOULD LIKE TO FEEL:

AS I COLOUR MY MANDALA, I FOCUS ON TIMES WHEN I FEEL HOW I WOULD LIKE TO FEEL. BY DOING THIS I ATTRACT MORE OF IT INTO MY FUTURE DAYS.

THE BEST THING THAT HAPPENED TODAY:

THINGS I ACCOMPLISHED TODAY, BIG AND SMALL:

TODAY'S DATE:

"Once you replace negative thoughts with positive ones, you'll start having positive results." —Willie Nelson

RIGHT NOW I FEEL:

I WOULD LIKE TO FEEL:

AS I COLOUR MY MANDALA, I FOCUS ON TIMES WHEN I FEEL HOW I WOULD LIKE TO FEEL. BY DOING THIS I ATTRACT MORE OF IT INTO MY FUTURE DAYS.

THE BEST THING THAT HAPPENED TODAY:

THINGS I ACCOMPLISHED TODAY, BIG AND SMALL:

TODAY'S DATE:

"Once you replace negative thoughts with positive ones, you'll start having positive results." — Willie Nelson

RIGHT NOW I FEEL:

I WOULD LIKE TO FEEL:

AS I COLOUR MY MANDALA, I FOCUS ON TIMES WHEN I FEEL HOW I WOULD LIKE TO FEEL. BY DOING THIS I ATTRACT MORE OF IT INTO MY FUTURE DAYS.

THE BEST THING THAT HAPPENED TODAY:

THINGS I ACCOMPLISHED TODAY, BIG AND SMALL:

TODAY'S DATE:

"Once you replace negative thoughts with positive ones, you'll start having positive results." — Willie Nelson

RIGHT NOW I FEEL:

I WOULD LIKE TO FEEL:

AS I COLOUR MY MANDALA, I FOCUS ON TIMES WHEN I FEEL HOW I WOULD LIKE TO FEEL. BY DOING THIS I ATTRACT MORE OF IT INTO MY FUTURE DAYS.

THE BEST THING THAT HAPPENED TODAY:

THINGS I ACCOMPLISHED TODAY, BIG AND SMALL:

TODAY'S DATE:

"Once you replace negative thoughts with positive ones, you'll start having positive results." — Willie Nelson

RIGHT NOW I FEEL:

I WOULD LIKE TO FEEL:

AS I COLOUR MY MANDALA, I FOCUS ON TIMES WHEN I FEEL HOW I WOULD LIKE TO FEEL. BY DOING THIS I ATTRACT MORE OF IT INTO MY FUTURE DAYS.

THE BEST THING THAT HAPPENED TODAY:

THINGS I ACCOMPLISHED TODAY, BIG AND SMALL:

TODAY'S DATE:

"Once you replace negative thoughts with positive ones, you'll start having positive results." — Willie Nelson

RIGHT NOW I FEEL:

I WOULD LIKE TO FEEL:

AS I COLOUR MY MANDALA, I FOCUS ON TIMES WHEN I FEEL HOW I WOULD LIKE TO FEEL. BY DOING THIS I ATTRACT MORE OF IT INTO MY FUTURE DAYS.

THE BEST THING THAT HAPPENED TODAY:

THINGS I ACCOMPLISHED TODAY, BIG AND SMALL:

TODAY'S DATE:

"Once you replace negative thoughts with positive ones, you'll start having positive results." — Willie Nelson

RIGHT NOW I FEEL:

I WOULD LIKE TO FEEL:

AS I COLOUR MY MANDALA, I FOCUS ON TIMES WHEN I FEEL HOW I WOULD LIKE TO FEEL. BY DOING THIS I ATTRACT MORE OF IT INTO MY FUTURE DAYS.

THE BEST THING THAT HAPPENED TODAY:

THINGS I ACCOMPLISHED TODAY, BIG AND SMALL:

TODAY'S DATE:

"Once you replace negative thoughts with positive ones, you'll start having positive results." — Willie Nelson

RIGHT NOW I FEEL:

I WOULD LIKE TO FEEL:

AS I COLOUR MY MANDALA, I FOCUS ON TIMES WHEN I FEEL HOW I WOULD LIKE TO FEEL. BY DOING THIS I ATTRACT MORE OF IT INTO MY FUTURE DAYS.

THE BEST THING THAT HAPPENED TODAY:

THINGS I ACCOMPLISHED TODAY, BIG AND SMALL:

TODAY'S DATE:

"Once you replace negative thoughts with positive ones, you'll start having positive results." —Willie Nelson

RIGHT NOW I FEEL:

I WOULD LIKE TO FEEL:

AS I COLOUR MY MANDALA, I FOCUS ON TIMES WHEN I FEEL HOW I WOULD LIKE TO FEEL. BY DOING THIS I ATTRACT MORE OF IT INTO MY FUTURE DAYS.

THE BEST THING THAT HAPPENED TODAY:

THINGS I ACCOMPLISHED TODAY, BIG AND SMALL:

TODAY'S DATE:

"Once you replace negative thoughts with positive ones, you'll start having positive results." — Willie Nelson

RIGHT NOW I FEEL:

I WOULD LIKE TO FEEL:

AS I COLOUR MY MANDALA, I FOCUS ON TIMES WHEN I FEEL HOW I WOULD LIKE TO FEEL. BY DOING THIS I ATTRACT MORE OF IT INTO MY FUTURE DAYS.

THE BEST THING THAT HAPPENED TODAY:

THINGS I ACCOMPLISHED TODAY, BIG AND SMALL:

TODAY'S DATE:

"Once you replace negative thoughts with positive ones, you'll start having positive results." — Willie Nelson

RIGHT NOW I FEEL:

I WOULD LIKE TO FEEL:

AS I COLOUR MY MANDALA, I FOCUS ON TIMES WHEN I FEEL HOW I WOULD LIKE TO FEEL. BY DOING THIS I ATTRACT MORE OF IT INTO MY FUTURE DAYS.

THE BEST THING THAT HAPPENED TODAY:

THINGS I ACCOMPLISHED TODAY, BIG AND SMALL:

TODAY'S DATE:

"Once you replace negative thoughts with positive ones, you'll start having positive results." — Willie Nelson

RIGHT NOW I FEEL:

I WOULD LIKE TO FEEL:

AS I COLOUR MY MANDALA, I FOCUS ON TIMES WHEN I FEEL HOW I WOULD LIKE TO FEEL. BY DOING THIS I ATTRACT MORE OF IT INTO MY FUTURE DAYS.

THE BEST THING THAT HAPPENED TODAY:

THINGS I ACCOMPLISHED TODAY, BIG AND SMALL:

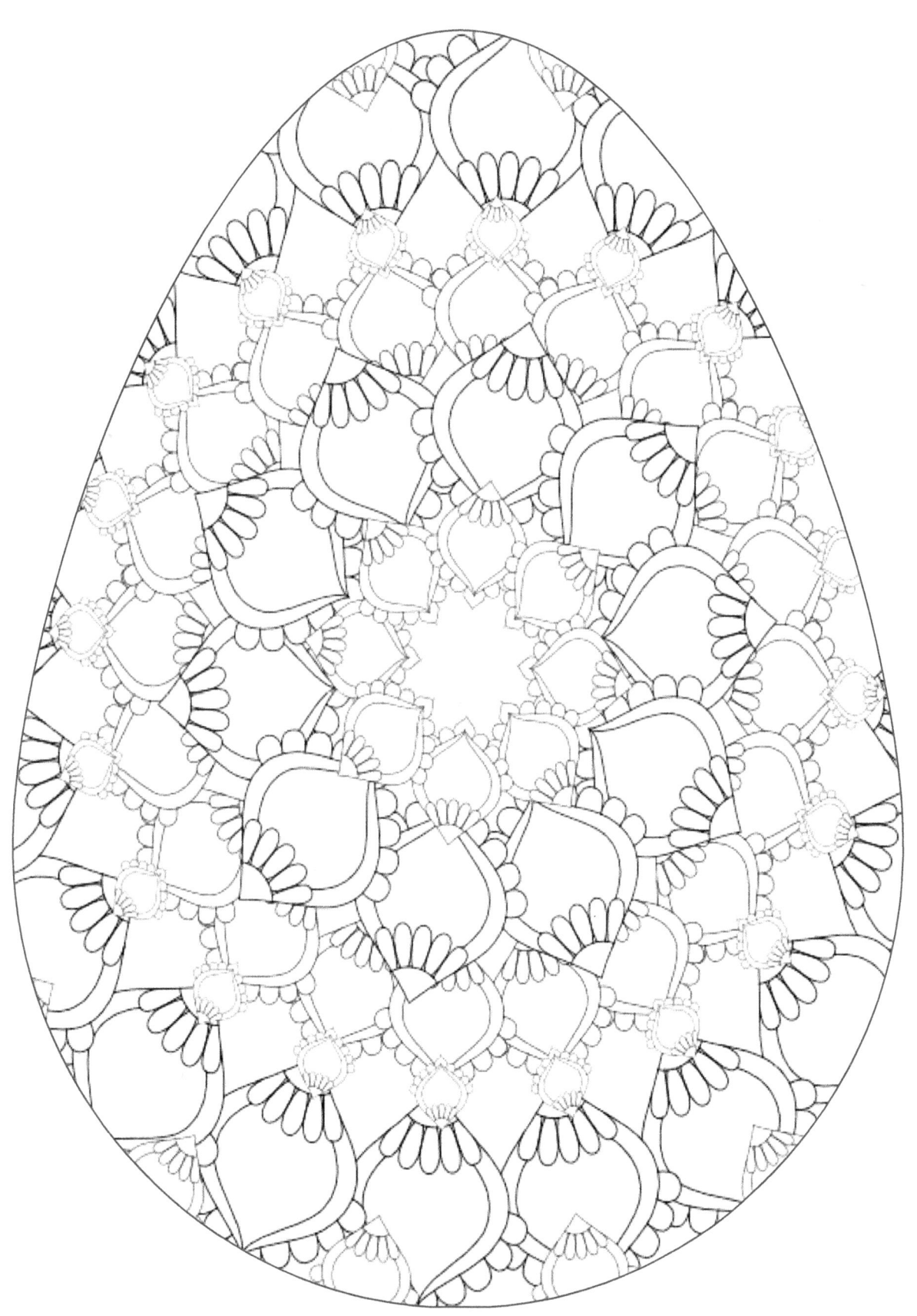

TODAY'S DATE:

"Once you replace negative thoughts with positive ones, you'll start having positive results." — Willie Nelson

RIGHT NOW I FEEL:

I WOULD LIKE TO FEEL:

AS I COLOUR MY MANDALA, I FOCUS ON TIMES WHEN I FEEL HOW I WOULD LIKE TO FEEL. BY DOING THIS I ATTRACT MORE OF IT INTO MY FUTURE DAYS.

THE BEST THING THAT HAPPENED TODAY:

THINGS I ACCOMPLISHED TODAY, BIG AND SMALL:

TODAY'S DATE:

"Once you replace negative thoughts with positive ones, you'll start having positive results." —Willie Nelson

RIGHT NOW I FEEL:

I WOULD LIKE TO FEEL:

AS I COLOUR MY MANDALA, I FOCUS ON TIMES WHEN I FEEL HOW I WOULD LIKE TO FEEL. BY DOING THIS I ATTRACT MORE OF IT INTO MY FUTURE DAYS.

THE BEST THING THAT HAPPENED TODAY:

THINGS I ACCOMPLISHED TODAY, BIG AND SMALL:

TODAY'S DATE:

"Once you replace negative thoughts with positive ones, you'll start having positive results." — Willie Nelson

RIGHT NOW I FEEL:

I WOULD LIKE TO FEEL:

AS I COLOUR MY MANDALA, I FOCUS ON TIMES WHEN I FEEL HOW I WOULD LIKE TO FEEL. BY DOING THIS I ATTRACT MORE OF IT INTO MY FUTURE DAYS.

THE BEST THING THAT HAPPENED TODAY:

THINGS I ACCOMPLISHED TODAY, BIG AND SMALL:

TODAY'S DATE:

"Once you replace negative thoughts with positive ones, you'll start having positive results." —Willie Nelson

RIGHT NOW I FEEL:

I WOULD LIKE TO FEEL:

AS I COLOUR MY MANDALA, I FOCUS ON TIMES WHEN I FEEL HOW I WOULD LIKE TO FEEL. BY DOING THIS I ATTRACT MORE OF IT INTO MY FUTURE DAYS.

THE BEST THING THAT HAPPENED TODAY:

THINGS I ACCOMPLISHED TODAY, BIG AND SMALL:

TODAY'S DATE:

"Once you replace negative thoughts with positive ones, you'll start having positive results." —Willie Nelson

RIGHT NOW I FEEL:

I WOULD LIKE TO FEEL:

AS I COLOUR MY MANDALA, I FOCUS ON TIMES WHEN I FEEL HOW I WOULD LIKE TO FEEL. BY DOING THIS I ATTRACT MORE OF IT INTO MY FUTURE DAYS.

THE BEST THING THAT HAPPENED TODAY:

THINGS I ACCOMPLISHED TODAY, BIG AND SMALL:

TODAY'S DATE:

"Once you replace negative thoughts with positive ones, you'll start having positive results." — Willie Nelson

RIGHT NOW I FEEL:

I WOULD LIKE TO FEEL:

AS I COLOUR MY MANDALA, I FOCUS ON TIMES WHEN I FEEL HOW I WOULD LIKE TO FEEL. BY DOING THIS I ATTRACT MORE OF IT INTO MY FUTURE DAYS.

THE BEST THING THAT HAPPENED TODAY:

THINGS I ACCOMPLISHED TODAY, BIG AND SMALL:

TODAY'S DATE:

"Once you replace negative thoughts with positive ones, you'll start having positive results." — Willie Nelson

RIGHT NOW I FEEL:

I WOULD LIKE TO FEEL:

AS I COLOUR MY MANDALA, I FOCUS ON TIMES WHEN I FEEL HOW I WOULD LIKE TO FEEL. BY DOING THIS I ATTRACT MORE OF IT INTO MY FUTURE DAYS.

THE BEST THING THAT HAPPENED TODAY:

THINGS I ACCOMPLISHED TODAY, BIG AND SMALL:

TODAY'S DATE:

"Once you replace negative thoughts with positive ones, you'll start having positive results." —Willie Nelson

RIGHT NOW I FEEL:

I WOULD LIKE TO FEEL:

AS I COLOUR MY MANDALA, I FOCUS ON TIMES WHEN I FEEL HOW I WOULD LIKE TO FEEL. BY DOING THIS I ATTRACT MORE OF IT INTO MY FUTURE DAYS.

THE BEST THING THAT HAPPENED TODAY:

THINGS I ACCOMPLISHED TODAY, BIG AND SMALL:

TODAY'S DATE:

"Once you replace negative thoughts with positive ones, you'll start having positive results." —Willie Nelson

RIGHT NOW I FEEL:

I WOULD LIKE TO FEEL:

AS I COLOUR MY MANDALA, I FOCUS ON TIMES WHEN I FEEL HOW I WOULD LIKE TO FEEL. BY DOING THIS I ATTRACT MORE OF IT INTO MY FUTURE DAYS.

THE BEST THING THAT HAPPENED TODAY:

THINGS I ACCOMPLISHED TODAY, BIG AND SMALL:

TODAY'S DATE:

"Once you replace negative thoughts with positive ones, you'll start having positive results." — Willie Nelson

RIGHT NOW I FEEL:

I WOULD LIKE TO FEEL:

AS I COLOUR MY MANDALA, I FOCUS ON TIMES WHEN I FEEL HOW I WOULD LIKE TO FEEL. BY DOING THIS I ATTRACT MORE OF IT INTO MY FUTURE DAYS.

THE BEST THING THAT HAPPENED TODAY:

THINGS I ACCOMPLISHED TODAY, BIG AND SMALL:

THE MONTH IN REVIEW

"ONCE YOU REPLACE NEGATIVE THOUGHTS WITH POSITIVE ONES, YOU'LL START HAVING POSITIVE RESULTS." — WILLIE NELSON

THINGS I ACCOMPLISHED BIG AND SMALL:

THE BEST THINGS THAT HAPPENED THIS MONTH:

THE MONTH IN REVIEW

NOTES TO SELF:

THE MONTH IN REVIEW

NOTES TO SELF:

www.ingramcontent.com/pod-product-compliance
Lightning Source LLC
Chambersburg PA
CBHW081455060426
42444CB00037BA/3282